Coral Reef

Inside Australia's Great Barrier Reef

Contents

Australia's Great Barrier Reef

It takes about an hour, travelling in a fast boat, to get to the Great Barrier Reef. From the boat, the coral of the reef looks like dark patches in the sea. In some places, waves break over the coral. In other places, coral sticks up above the surface of the sea, like brown, knobbly rocks.

The Great Barrier Reef is in the Coral Sea off the north-east coast of Australia. It is the largest group of coral reefs and islands in the world.

This is what a coral reef looks like from high above the water.

This is what a coral reef looks
like under the water.

The coral reef is like an amazing underwater garden. It is covered in strange, beautiful shapes and brilliant colours. The coral has grown into mounds and steep-sided cliffs. Bright fish dart everywhere. Sea anemones wave their tentacles. Sea snakes rest amongst the coral.

In some places, the coral grows near the surface of the water. Where the sea is deeper, coral-covered cliffs lead down to the dark ocean depths.

People cannot see many colours deep down in the sea because there is very little light. But as soon as a bright light is shone onto the reef, all the brilliant colours of the coral can be seen.

Coral

What is coral?

Coral can be feathery or rubbery or spiky. It has many different shapes. Coral can look like a rock, or a plant. But coral is an animal, and it eats other animals.

The coral animal is very small. It is called a polyp. A polyp is a soft bag, with a stomach and a mouth. The mouth is surrounded by arms called tentacles. These tentacles can sting other animals.

Some coral polyps are so small that you can hardly see them. Most are about this size.

This polyp has closed up its tentacles.

These polyps have opened out their tentacles.

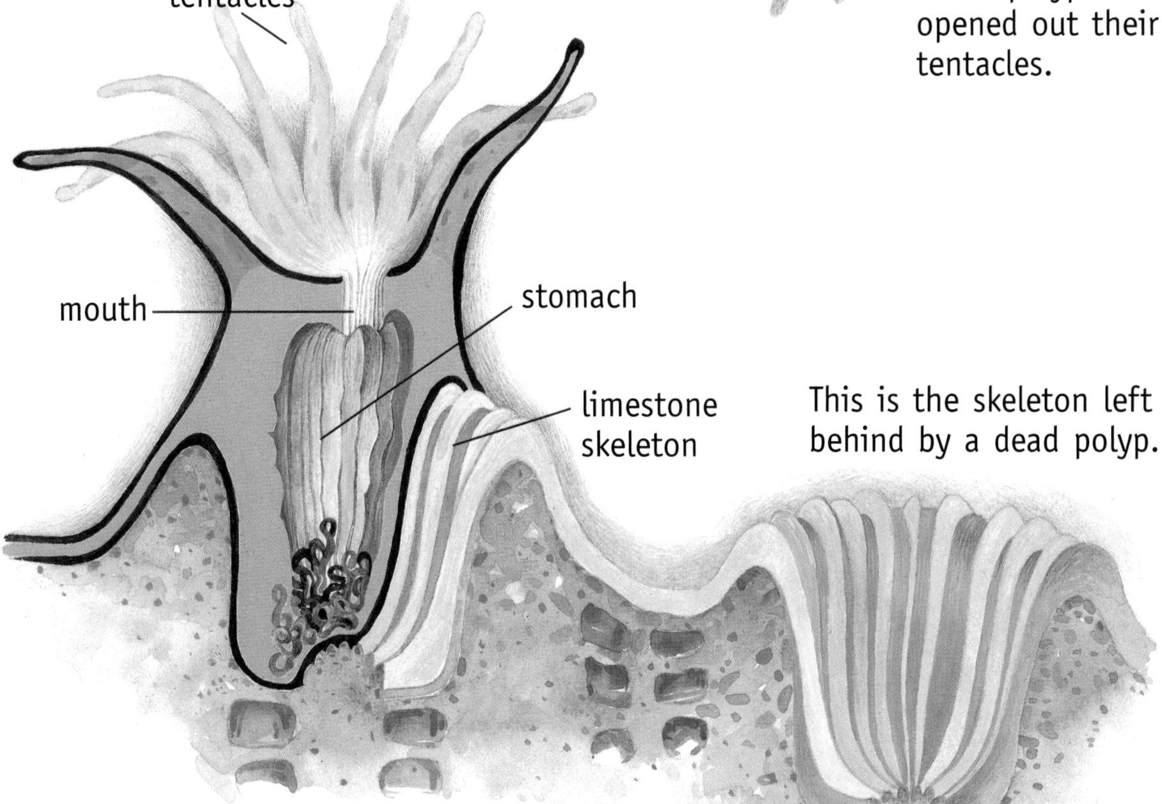

tentacles

mouth

stomach

limestone skeleton

This is the skeleton left behind by a dead polyp.

Coral cannot move around to find its food because it is stuck in one place. Tiny animals float past in the sea. If they bump into a polyp's tentacles, they are stung and caught. The tentacles put the food into the polyp's mouth.

A large coral is made up of many polyps, all exactly the same. The polyps are joined to each other and so the food that goes into one polyp's mouth helps to feed all the other polyps too.

The polyp's tentacles have come out to find food.

There are many different kinds of corals on the Barrier Reef. Some are soft and some are hard.

Soft corals look velvety and delicate as they sway in the water, but many of them are poisonous. Very few animals eat soft corals.

Hard corals have skeletons. Each polyp skeleton looks a bit like a cup.

How is a coral reef formed?

When the polyps of hard corals die, they leave their skeletons behind. New polyps grow on top of the old skeletons. So the coral gets slowly bigger and bigger. Only the polyps on the outer surface of the coral are alive and brightly coloured. Underneath the living polyps, the coral is white and dead.

Coral reefs are made from millions and millions of tiny polyps and millions and millions of their old skeletons.

Tiny plants live inside the coral polyps of the Great Barrier Reef. These tiny plants, called 'zooxanthellae', help the coral to grow.

Corals on the Barrier Reef need to grow in sea-water that is

- not too deep
- warm
- clean
- clear

Part of a coral mound has been cut away to show the dead coral.

The Great Barrier Reef is not one huge reef. It is made up of 2,900 different coral reefs.

Some corals grow about 2 centimetres a year. Some can grow 10 centimetres a year. The coral reefs of the Great Barrier Reef have been growing for thousands of years.

This is what the Barrier Reef looks like from the air.

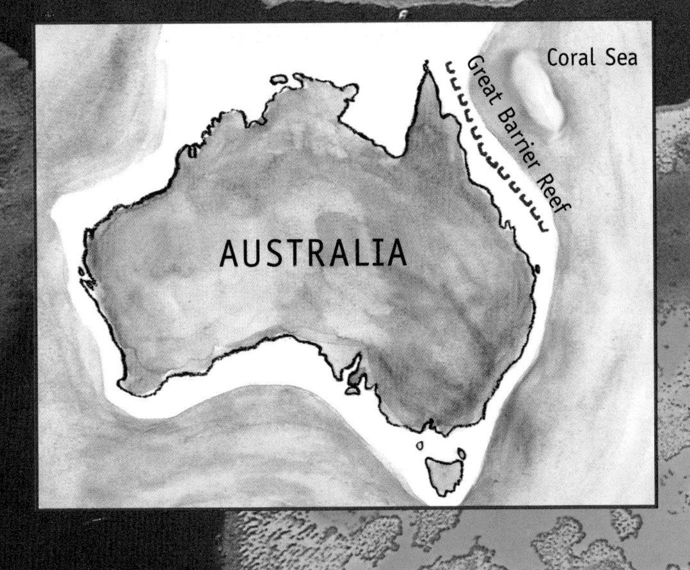

How does a new coral begin?

Many corals on the Great Barrier Reef spawn on the same few nights of the year, in early summer. The corals spawn when the moon is shining and the sea is calm.

Suddenly, the water is filled with tiny coloured balls – red, pink, orange, blue – all floating upwards. The balls have come from the mouths of the coral polyps. As the balls reach the surface of the sea, they break open and release coral eggs.

1

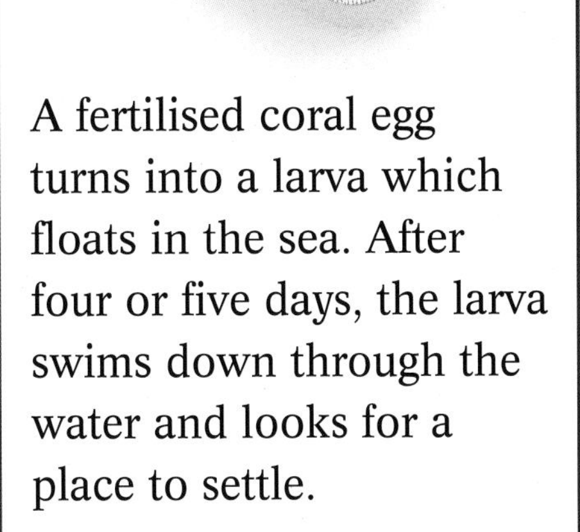

A fertilised coral egg turns into a larva which floats in the sea. After four or five days, the larva swims down through the water and looks for a place to settle.

2

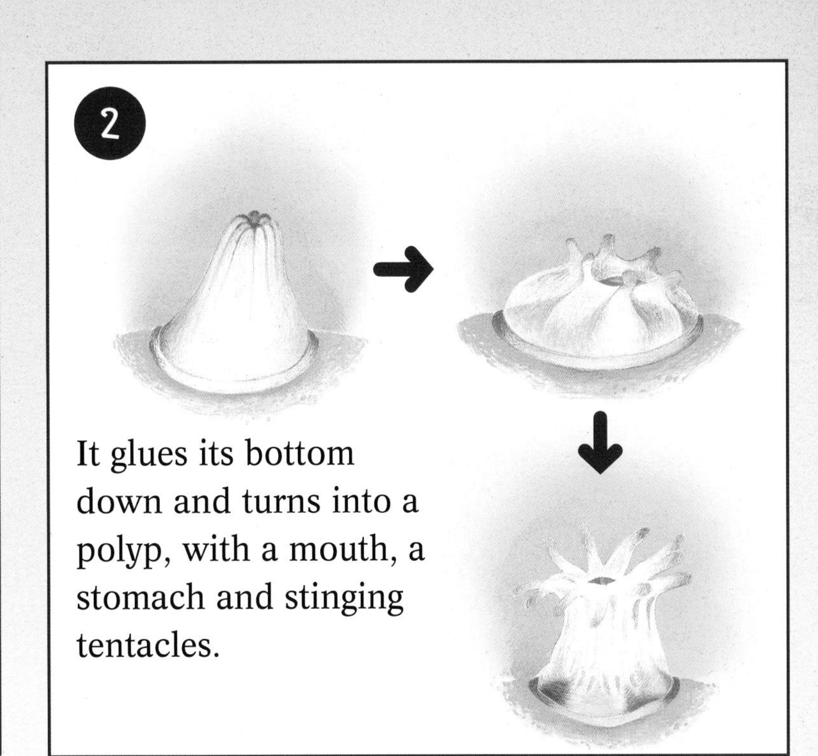

It glues its bottom down and turns into a polyp, with a mouth, a stomach and stinging tentacles.

3

After a few months, the new polyp produces another polyp just like itself,

4

then another and another.

5

After a year, the new coral might be 2 centimetres big, made up of about thirty polyps.

6

Years later, on a warm, moonlit night, this coral will also spawn and tiny new corals will begin to grow somewhere else.

Animals of the coral reef

Animals that attack coral

This blue-green parrot fish hangs in the water, eating coral.

Parrot fish

Parrot fish have strong teeth which are joined together to make a kind of beak. Very few animals can crunch up hard coral, but the parrot fish can.

At night, parrot fish make themselves a cocoon to sleep in. The cocoon looks like a see-through sleeping-bag.

Crown of thorns starfish

Crown of thorns starfish creep onto coral. The starfish pull their own stomachs out through their mouths. The stomachs spread over the coral and dissolve the polyps into 'polyp soup'. Only the little coral skeletons are left.

Crown of thorns starfish can grow as big as bicycle wheels. When they attack a reef, they cause a great deal of damage.

Most starfish have five arms, but crown of thorns starfish have up to twenty-one arms which are covered in sharp, poisonous spines. People used to try to kill the dreaded crown of thorns by tearing it into pieces. They did not know that they were making new starfish by doing this. If a starfish arm has a bit of body left on it then it can grow into a new starfish.

Crown of thorns starfish usually live for about ten years. In that time, a female starfish can produce up to 700 million eggs.

Cleaning stations

Some animals on the reef help and protect each other.

Little shrimps wait beside a large coral, waving their long antennae. A fish swims up, but it does not eat the shrimps because this is a 'cleaning station'.

The shrimps nibble at the fish, eating the tiny animals and fungi that are on its skin. The shrimps clean the fish and, at the same time, have a meal. In return, the fish does not eat the shrimps.

Some small fish work as 'cleaners' too. They swim right inside the mouth of a big fish to clean its teeth.

'Cleaner' shrimps and fish also help turtles and stingrays. 'Cleaners' are very important to the health of many animals on the reef.

Colours and patterns

Reef fish have amazing colours and patterns, but no-one really knows why. The fish are trying not to be eaten. Perhaps their colours and patterns camouflage them and help to protect them.

At night, fish hide in cracks and caves to sleep. Some brightly coloured fish can change their bright colours to dull colours. Perhaps this helps the fish to hide during the night.

Many poisonous fish have very bright colours and patterns. Perhaps these colours and patterns are a warning that the fish are not good to eat. This poisonous fish is a puffer fish.

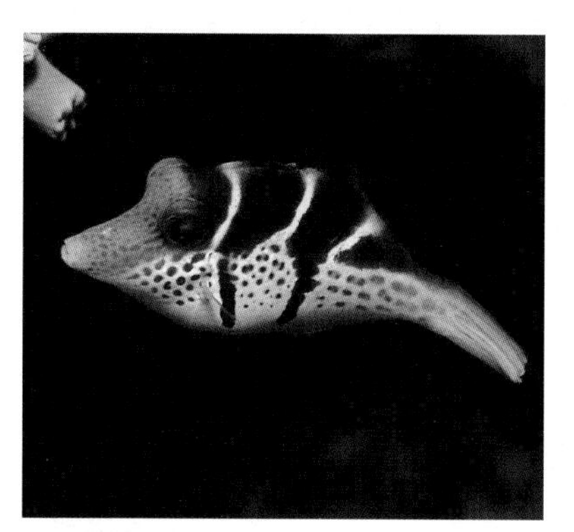

Some fish which are not poisonous copy the colour patterns of poisonous fish so that they look dangerous. This harmless fish is a leatherjacket.

Anemones, sea squirts and Christmas tree worms

Anemones look like pretty flowers but they are animals. They have stings on their tentacles which help them to catch their food.

Some animals use stinging anemones to protect themselves.

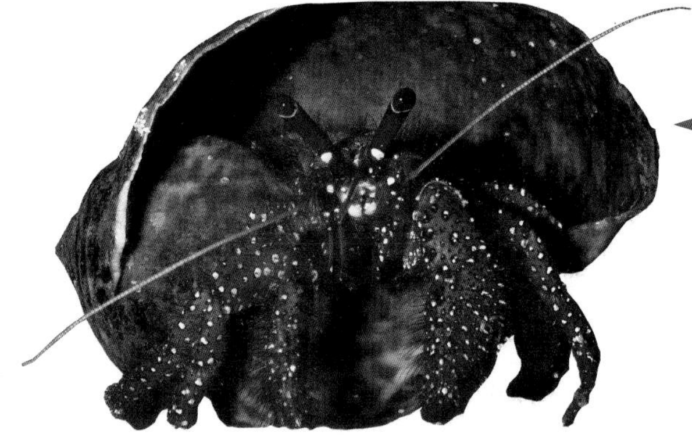

Hermit crabs take over seashells and live in them. Some hermit crabs carry stinging anemones on top of their shell homes as extra protection.

The boxer crab carries anemones in its claws and pushes them at attackers.

Sea slugs have amazing colours. One kind of sea slug eats coral and sea anemones. The slug takes their stinging parts out and stores them inside spiky bits on its back. The slug uses the stings to defend itself from its enemies.

Sea cucumbers are animals which crawl along, looking a bit like big rubbery sausages. One kind of sea cucumber can turn itself into a squidgy liquid if it is picked up. When it is left alone again, it pulls itself back into its usual shape.

Sea squirts are animals which stick themselves onto rocks or coral.

Sponges look like plants but they are living animals. They pump water through their bodies, taking out tiny bits of food that are in the water.

Many animals shelter inside live coral. Christmas tree worms poke their feathery tentacles outside the coral to feed, but pull back inside the coral for safety.

Giant clams can live for about thirty years.

Venomous animals

Many of the animals which live on the coral reef are venomous. They have a poison, called 'venom', which they can use to catch their prey. They can also use their venom to stop other animals from eating them.

Stonefish

A stonefish lies on the seabed, looking just like a knobbly rock. It waits for shrimps or small fish to swim past, opens its mouth and sucks them in very fast.

The stonefish has thirteen spines along its back. If anything presses on the stonefish then a terrible venom shoots up the spines. The stonefish is the world's most venomous fish.

Cone shells

Cone shells look pretty, but they have a venomous tooth on the end of their feeding tube which can kill a person.

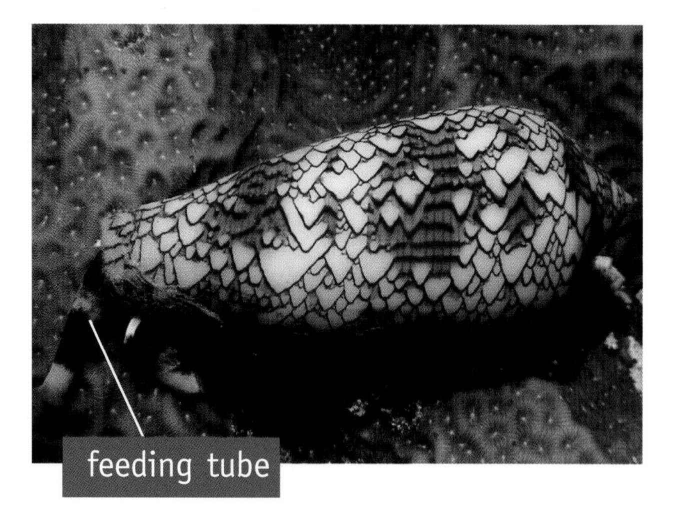

Box jellyfish

A box jellyfish floats in the water, trailing its long stinging tentacles. The box jellyfish feeds on shrimps, which are stung and killed when they bump into the jellyfish's tentacles.

The box jellyfish's stings can also kill people. Even a bit of tentacle that has broken off the jellyfish can still sting anything it touches.

Blue-ringed octopus

The blue-ringed octopus has a very small body, but its venom can also kill people.

Blue-ringed octopuses live in shallow water and rock pools. Sometimes, they climb inside empty drink cans and bottles.

Sharks

Some of the small, venomous animals are much more dangerous than sharks. But people are very frightened of sharks.

Small sharks, like the blacktip, swim in shallow water where they catch fish, squid and sea snakes to eat.

Tiger sharks usually hunt on the edge of the reef near cliffs of coral, but sometimes they swim in shallow water.

Tiger sharks hunt turtles, seabirds, other sharks and mammals. They eat whatever they can find. Tin cans, boots, a handbag, a car number plate, have all been found in the stomachs of tiger sharks.

Catsharks and wobbegongs are slow-moving sharks that swim along the sandy bottom of the coral reef, looking for crabs and shellfish. This is a wobbegong.

Adult blacktips are about 1.5 metres (150 centimetres) long.

Adult tiger sharks are over 5 metres long.

Green turtles

Sometimes, the small round heads of green turtles appear above the water. Then the turtles dive down again to feed on seagrass and algae.

Green turtles grow very slowly and can live for over a hundred years. The females are more than forty years old when they lay their first eggs.

The females lay their eggs in the sand on island beaches. After about two months, the young turtles break out of the eggs and burrow up through the sand. This is hard work and it takes them about seven days to reach the surface. Then they hurry towards the sea. Birds, crabs, sharks and fish are waiting to catch them.

Dugongs and whales

Dugongs

Dugongs swim along the sandy bottom of the sea, slowly munching the waving green seagrass. Every minute or so, they come up to the surface to breathe.

The Barrier Reef is one of the few places in the world where dugongs live and look after their young.

Humpback whales

Every winter, humpback whales swim back to the Barrier Reef from Antarctica, where they have been feeding all summer. The female whales give birth to their young in the warm waters of the coral reef.

Wrecks

This is the anchor from the wreck of HMS *Pandora,* which sank near Raine Island in 1791.

It is sometimes difficult to see that there is coral growing just below the surface of the sea. This is very dangerous for sailors because sharp coral can easily tear holes in the side of a ship.

Hundreds of ships lie wrecked along the Great Barrier Reef. Fish and octopuses live inside the ships' dark, broken hulls. Cannons, china plates, and coins have spilt out across the seabed. Coral and seaweed grow over the ships' anchors.

Some of the ships sank with treasure on board – chests of money, bags of gold. But all the wrecks are important and need to be protected because people study them to learn about the past. They can find out from the wrecks how the ships were built and how they were used.

Islands of the coral reef

Waves sweep along the reefs, carrying broken pieces of coral and little bits of dead plants and animals. Sometimes, these bits and pieces come together on a flat part of the reef and make an island, called a coral cay.

Many coral cays are just sand banks, like small beaches in the middle of the sea. Beautiful shells lie everywhere on the thick sand of the cays.

Sometimes, in a big storm, all the sand is washed away.

Thousands of seabirds nest on coral cays. Most of the birds lay their eggs straight onto the sand because there are no land animals here which might steal the birds' eggs and chicks.

Many of the birds which come to the coral cays bring seeds on their feathers. Sometimes, floating seeds are washed up onto the sand. Creepers, bushes, and even trees, start to grow from these seeds on some of the coral cays.

Protecting the Great Barrier Reef

Every part of a coral reef has things living in it and on it. Animals fight and kill each other for space and food. Coral reefs are complicated places where every part depends on every other part.

Coral reefs are fragile places. They can easily be damaged. They need to be protected, and understood.

The Great Barrier Reef is the largest collection of coral reefs in the world. Every year, more and more people visit the Great Barrier Reef. Scientists are studying the reef to find out about this huge and wonderful maze of reefs and islands, filled with plants and animals.

The Great Barrier Reef is now a World Heritage Site, which helps to protect it.

Coral reefs can be damaged by

- storms breaking them
- animals eating them
- people walking on them
- diving equipment knocking into them
- ships' anchors dropping onto them
- people taking away too many reef fish and animals from them
- people polluting the water with oil spills, sewage and fertilisers
- rivers washing mud into the sea

Index